S0-BDG-261

MAKING THE GOOD

MAKING THE GOOD

Julia Connor

julia connor.

Tooth of Time
Books
1988

Copyright © 1988, Julia Connor
Cover photograph copyright © 1988 by Julia Connor.

ACKNOWLEDGEMENTS

The author wishes to acknowledge the generous help of
Jim Anderson, Sabra Basler and Diane di Prima in preparing
the manuscript.

Some of the poems in this book first appeared in: *Landing Signals,
An Anthology of Sacramento Poets* (1985); *Quercus,* v. 3, #2; *Poet News;
Pinchpenny.*

The following poems have appeared as broadsides: "The Place of
Dark Blue Flowers," "Winter Pentecost," "Who Brings Down
Water," "Hathor's Bells," "Temple Guard."

Cover art "Goddess Figure," ceramic, 8½ × 5", Julia Connor,
Collection of Diane di Prima.

ISBN: 0-940510-16-2

CONTENTS

to legomenoux . . . to dromenon
(things said are things done)

for M. C.

ONE

THE PLACE OF DARK BLUE FLOWERS

This light of autumn's
whose arms fall
in random strands
her tattered dress
caught on the curb

> "O Lady," I said
> "your legs, I mean
> the language of your foot
> is caught
> just here
>
> Are you alone tonight?"
>
> "No," she said. "Music
> is right behind me."

She is the river
music trails

her thighs
the bridges

men cast
lines from.

Dusk lit
as we walked

and she said
call me

> "Sacramento."

Ripe
from her tongue

it fell into a swollen song
behind her.

Night
kissed

and lilies
sprang from her abdomen

slung low,
a delta

riding down
the flute of her limbs.

She is all limb
this lady.

                    *

She is elf tongue
whose dress I gather scraps of

whose mouth
is the cave

bison horns
were drawn upon

until the beast came
of its own accord

and dancers
stomped their feet

at the entrance
of her beginning

where men
blew ocher dust

thru hollow tubes
printing their hands

embedding them
into her stone cunt.

        *

She, the wide-hipped
bell-skirted one

we found in Spain
walks here

still glorious
in her disheveled gown

       "O Lady," I said
       "Your stars hold
       such promise!"

for they spilt as she bent
to gather shadow

       "O Dark One," I called, "you appear
       in this light
              so like a girl."

But she had turned south
towards the boats in the harbor

and the hem of her dress
cut a path as she moved

thru the place
of dark blue flowers.

MICHAELMAS

Fire you season
you red-leafed vine
licking the darkness
Godwards.

In time weather suggests script
                              pulse
                              temperament
                              tide.

Fevers made manifest
like fondnesses gone physical
and pressed into matter.

All forms
form.

> "What we are looking for
> is that which is looking,"
> Saint Francis said.

Iron in the ground
on the page a stroke
or lightning over the barley field
COUNTENANCES
flaming face forward
into seed.

WINTER PENTECOST

This sympathy
could be an angel we share
    who backed against the wall
        drops arms
    as if there never were

        nor could be again

        any wars

Or,
        it could be a woman of the moon
a kind of idea made pregnant
        by our presence

I mean this Flame-Bride
who weds us in the moment when
        we change the world
and speak
        in tongues.

LIKE SATURN

For Diane di Prima

Like Saturn, Diane
I was night-walking the American
when it came to me (whatever Olson says)
we ARE born of this MERE craft.

The voice slid down the rapids
knocking stars out of water/orbiting
it's dizzying to look up
nothing's safe and I knew
the house was gone.
The small storm had aimed itself.
My blood ached and as the walls went down
I tried to remember the names that margin
the Michaelmas script:
      Antares
      Spica
      Aldebaran.   How on Halloween
the heart-star tries to line up
with the Sun.

So it is a measuring and a given
that faces origin.   That's emblematic.
And walking where I had slept
I saw the Angel Spin
(the potter's wheel) my foot knows
as well as my hand.
Some jar perhaps?   Or a disc?
Or just some exercise the sky needs.

The pots that keep the kitchen warm
when no one's eating.
  Via intention, then
those storms foretold by old bones
or the poem coming in;
  a huge woman in tiny shoes
tottering,
   we throw our pots.

It may well be the problem is too vast
or the mind unsteady. Every red anemone
is swoon before actual flower.
Yes, and my voice may have been an owl
marauding the night
where ablaze in the stream I saw
an old resistance turn on itself
igniting the fire in lead.

EPITAPH

Language who as a woman I saw
undress her lovely limbs
became my intimate
became a poetess
whose wide dream swept over me
whose thigh upon my own
was moist, was prest
where the wild sea grew calm
and I was the narrow shore
in waves she came upon.

TWO

ON THE MOON OF THE HARE

It was known as
the Moon of Eostre,
Moon of the Hare
mascot of she who was
Lady of Byblos
Egypt's Hathor
Demeter of Mycenae
Aphrodite of Cyprus
who the Old Testament
calls Asherah/Ashtoreth
the one Solomon adored
and whose name itself
meant "sacred grove."

From Sumerian seals of 2300 B.C.
she stares and squats
on her consort's body
to manifest the Triple of love and death
the moment-in-turning,
the Kali
of interior self.

She is called Astroarche
Queen of the Heavens
who would bestow
the astral light of stars
on all beloved children.
She is Astarte.
Before Isis.
Before Sophia.
Before Mary.

It unwinds into mystery
this first Sunday after
the first full moon of Spring
as a dark entrance
that resurrects the memory,
Yoni of divine groves
and sacred origin.

It is to Asherah
as Aphrodite-Mari
that Adonis the beautiful returns
gored in the groin
by the Goddess's boar-masked priest
flowering where his blood falls
at the hye-tide of the red anemone
that he may be called Lord,
the castrated one,
the sacrificed-savior-God.
It is he that Jerusalem
will later name Tammuz
saying he was born in a cave
of the virgin, Myrrh-of-the-Sea.

Or as Anchises
his severed organ
will become the Son,
the ithyphallic Priapus,
to be known as Osiris-Min in Egypt,
Eros in Greece.
Priapus who bears the pruning knife
as sign of what must be done
before new life appears.

For it is said he reaps the grain
and sprouts anew from the womb
in clay pots called "kernos"
"the gardens of Adonis"
who is dead but will rise again
out of a cave that Luke
will later describe, (23:53)
". . . wherein never before man was laid."

For Tammuz is
Dumuzi/Damu of Sumer
their 'only begotton son'
the "Son of Blood"
who fertilized the earth
where he bled
and was called Heavenly Shepherd,
was sacrificed in the form of a lamb
and attended by women who wailed
. . . the man of wisdom,
    the man of sorrow,
    why have they slain . . . ?

He it was for whom the Jews
named a month of their calendar
and he again who became Usirsir
generative of Osiris
keeper of the flocks of the dead
until the New Testament
transformed his name into Greek
and called him Thomas,
as a later angry church would curse him
"Hell's ambassador to Spain."
He, whose name had meant
Christos,
the anointed one.

*

The old calendar of thirteen
twenty-eight day months
from which comes our expression
"a year and a day"
was based on a knowledge of the menses
the woman's menstrual cycle
as the Moon-Mother spent the night
in each of her twenty-eight homes
where consorts attended her.
The old moon worshippers of Chaldea
legendary home of the father Abraham
transplanted their lunar months
to the ancient Hebrews,
to Egypt, northern Europe
Greece and Rome
where Latin kings were sacrificed
at the three day dark of the moon
called Ides
to assure the return of the Goddess
from the underworld
as even today our moveable feasts
drift through the canonical calendar
and are set by equinox and moon.

*

It may have been Saint Jerome
who first called Mary
Stella-Maris, Star of the Sea,
she who would be the one
to Christ-en Him
and who would appear
with yet other Marys

to include the one called Magdalene
whose name means
"she of the temple tower"
for it is said there were three
there were three Marys
standing at the cross
as once the three fates had stood
at the base of Odin's sacrificial tree.
The "white Mary" the early Welsh
named her in her triple form
and it is she the Gothic Cathedrals
would entitle Notre Dame
collectively called "Our Ladies"
or, "Palaces of the Queen of Heaven"
while at Chartres the one they called black
the "Virgio Paritua,"
"Virgin About to Give Birth"
was preserved in a crypt
and the French called her
Notre Dame Sous Terre,
Blessed Lady Under Ground.

Here, too, in the fifteenth century
a statue would appear
known as "La Vierge Ouvrante"
and would open to show a mother
who contained Jesus, God,
angels and saints
inside her.

So strong was the cult of Mary
that Gnostic gospels proclaim
it was women who announced
the resurrection
the men having been barred
from the mystery
because they were unprepared
as is echoed later in John (chapter 20, verse 9)
". . . They knew not the scriptures
              that he must rise again
              from the dead."

And it was Magdalene
they called "Mary Lucifer"
Mary the Light Giver
and whom Origen named
"the Mother of us all"
and from whom it is said
Christ exorcised the seven devils.
It is she we are told
who anointed Him for burial
pouring precious unguent
on his head.
This is the Magdalene
who retires to Marseilles
living for thirty eyars
without food or drink
and sustained by a nourishment
she terms "delightful"
and takes in through the ear.
And it is only she
the Pistis Sophia reminds us
that Christ ever addresses
as "Dearly Beloved"

she, whose bones were said to be found
in a cave called Saint Baume in Provence
where that name means
"holy tree."

And Sophia in Latin
was Sapientia
"spirit of feminine wisdom,"
and was seen in the form
of the dove of Aphrodite.
It is Sophia that Irenaeus names
"Mother of the Seven Planetary Spirits"
and she also that the Clementine Homilies
will proclaim as the union of Consort
and Son of Man
to reveal an androgynous God
whose male aspect is named Savior
and whose female is
Mother of All.
In the Cabala
she will be called the Shekina,
visible manifestation
of God
and of her the Gnostics will say
". . . the world soul
        was born of her smile."

                *

It runs deep in us
this ancient Will to recognize
what dies in order to become.
To celebrate the many in the One
that will receive the host
with the flowering rod
who, in the agony of what she knows
will bring forth
a divine child of the Sun.

She of the Virgin's Milk
wears also the name of both
Spirit and Bride of the Apocalypse.
She, of whom it was said
". . . And let him that is athirst come."

It runs deep
this quest to unwind the shroud
that would bind the wound
that would mark us with blood
at the hye-tide of the red anemone
this first Sunday after
the first full moon of Spring,
that would call us back
to the origin of things
and would have us see
in the turning point of time
a reflection of the moon
in the redemption
of Love.

L'OR RENTÉ

Out of the dream:

    "It is the research of all things
    by the composition of waters
    we seek in union . . ."

But I could not recognize the text
    and the voice fled though I knew
    it had worked me toward an end.
                    Metals appeared
        and a collage of medallions
           on which faces formed then bled
     into mountains
that turned as if the rim of the thing
were a wheel
        moving across fixed points and
                  yet still.
    Where it rested in his hand
it made a globe of light
       and fearing he might leave
I leapt forward and said
            "speak.
        You are the rose —
torn gold through which the image bleeds."

    O Archai   by night
    where your theater enters my poem
    a bright cock of dialogue
    driving forward our womanly souls

my hand falls back against your thigh
    as my child's body once fell into sleep
    feeling bigger than life

to enter a dark   beyond desire
    where confusion at work in her art
    lay buried
          a furious youth.

Sweet genius of speech
where from the well of center you rise
to secrete the vow of morning

a star is spun in the slumbering limb.

How alike to the promise of dream
you lay concealed in the eye
of the actor who would impersonate
your fullness of being

shy Raphael,
Angel
do you risk me again
(moon child I am and subject
to she who rides where sea breaks wild)

to writhe on your organ?

Bright serpent,
become again my tongue
for we still do not know
if Eve has been made
from a rib or a tail.

And upon waking we became the couple of the dream
though it all seemed to have happened earlier now.

Hermes go back
you have come too soon.
This is no spring.

But he would only smile
"Relax," he said, "we're a cycle.
You have remembered my breath."

And yes. Something like that
had flown past.

GOAT SONG

You whisper
                    goatherd
and I have come again
          the stone of the field is cold
          where eyes meet
we recognize the season.
It is winter
   I have walked toward you from the ledge
       where nothing is recorded
       the path invisible into the meadow
            the snow accepting my step
          the drag of my leg drawn
          over frozen surfaces.

The Kings have gone on ahead.

          Shepherd,
                    sweet song
       what thin air bonds us
   where no herb grows
          and all but the dark seems abandoned?
What music have we promise of here?
                    What epiphany?

I have seen them laid waste in the crevices
     all rock
   but for the white of their bones.
No pipe song intrudes.
                    No pasture
   and the moon hangs over the eternal grief.
One cannot tell what yet remains
     in the slow return of things done wrong
     nor measure the fireless hills
where even the bells of the bindweed
                    lie silent.

23

What news
                    poet,
sweet astride the night flute
        that stirs the beast to gather in these drifts
what news of the jar?
    What trail has Caspar left
        that words
    swifter than ourselves
        might fall upon
                            this whiff of myrrh?

THREE

MAKING THE GOOD

Beloved   I have come again
to beg of the night
    this hour

       to search the small and tapered light
            even now my hand is reaching toward
            some desperate ground   some sword

    wherefrom
a restless thing cries out
as if all of Love had fallen
    while we slept and would have me rise
    to stir her net of flame.

    Here
in the dim light by darkness cast
you flow thru the shaft of my pen
onto the ground of a poetry where
astride the white and wild Mother
    we are   making the good.

COLL

With the ninth lunation
the nutting moon
the hazel is the poet's tree

nine being sacred
to the Muses Calliope, Clio
Urania, Erato, Euterpe
Melpomene, Polyhumania
Thalia, Terpsichore.

Who are they
in the fruiting of
white magic's
mother
tree of the divining rod

whose memory we eat
in her ninth year?

And if the moon slides in
a white owl
whose cold eye we see
in her tall shadow

crisp, silent
worn.
Were there horns?

What hag brings autumn?
What star appears

then leaves
whose absence stings the dawn
so that birds take quicker flight?

Who stays
beside the candle flame
probing the night
to divine the one
who thought she went unseen?

Is it true what they say
of Connla's Well
over which nine hazels hung
to feed salmon a poetry
making them bright with color
so that never
wisdom and beauty
be found apart?

What device is this?
What art?
What spiraled measure
bids follow
September?

What light speaks the name?
What question can be asked?
And if suddenly her hounds appeared
would Necessity feed them?

Does she still tell tales
of Mac Coll, Mac Ceacht, Mac Greine
how all three mount the Triple-mare
binding Hazel, Plough and Sun?

Can one ask of love
in trepidation of her keening?

And if one were to trust the spell
and whisper

> "Hecate, sweet weird,
> you are welcome for the night"

would she bind the moon
and make the babies wail?

EPIPHANY

Poet
put down
your pen

become silent
like a woman
like a worm.

Become
all who have been
despised

let no one hear
the earth you move.

Dim star
few follow
be veil, be shroud.

Be dust.
Be the risen
scorpion.

WHO BRINGS DOWN WATER

So much time
is spent hauling

sticks,
old stones.

Even the poem
is carrion.

Behind the muse
is a mountain

and the man
who brings

her water
down.

HATHOR'S BELLS

For M. C.

About her are things
in no rush to divulge
the secret of
their ways

I have seen night
smudge her cheek
& angelic hands
pour dawn's milky glaze

into Love's own bovine eye

       always
       with the question:
       Is this bright enough,
       O Valentine?

O HOLY COW!
What can I say?

That she has become
a Maker-of-Bells
because function just is
that romantic

that the din of Her fields
as she goes past
  heads that lift
  udders that twitch

are just an orchestra
  (O sweet and lovely girls)!
at play
on Hathor's bells.

HIDDEN RELIGIONS

*"One might say each clump is the center
of a node from which* excursions *radiate
in various directions."*
                              Diane di Prima

Along the Boyne river, New Grange, Ireland
circa (who knows?) 3000 B.C.
spirals on the cap stones of dolmens
once covered by mounds
project an unbroken line

                    the triple swirl
                    that will haunt all Celtic art.

The Hill of the Witch stands
close by.

Mega Lithos, great stone, says nothing
but stands, a sign, a clearing in the woods
the mark of a reciprocity
between the seen and unseen divine
for the Spirit the stone possesses
becomes, in turn, the SpiritLand
where at sunrise on winter solstice
a shaft of light enters the apse
penetrates her dark hall
and comes to rest
in the libation bowl
at the rear.

Here, dancing on the line where history
becomes myth
we meet Darkness as Temple
thru which the bright cock shines

so,
my own tide rises
to meet the light
in a lover's eye.

To see measure as a knotting of cords
is to enter the dance
                    "who danceth not, knows not
                    what is being done" Christ said

We do not know
who sang down these stones
that tune geography with time
this Temanos,
now called Mystery Center
in which the act of love was rite

but we know magic to be exact:
that energy is drawn to the path
imagination makes for it
and the body
follows that.

Pound's dictum:
                    "If it's worth writing
                    it's worth carving in stone"

is but the poet's drive
to dig deep into matter
to write as if words could haul
megaliths
                    each breath chipped and fitted
                    to the corbelled vault
                    wherein the Beloved
                    lies.

FOUR

RIVER ELEGY

1.

I am so familiar here
that wild grasses bend,
the river passes quietly,
bare trees hold their boughs
apart.

No bird sings
no fish surfaces
where I have come.

Where I have come
no love enraptures me,
no God is torn apart,
no breath pretends to be the first or last,
no line of art becomes
my plan.

No presence changes
or is changed by me
and yet I am
too much among men

2.

Upon the river's morning brow
still and serpentine she comes
arousing the bird
to light the slough-grass flag
where the dark and silent ones
circle at her stem.

3.

What current the Dark god swims
that only Wound reflects

    and fallen
    as if from song estranged

    returns
    a mute and swollen thing

what wing
swept this early bud
to his mad stream?

4.

Dark One
forgive my eyes
that seek you
in water.

Forgive my hand
trembling now
over the moment
past.

HELEN

for H.D.

Where she was most ardent

small birds perched

for the love of which
she became woman;

slipped from her sandals

and lit braziers
on a beach.

AS MELISSAE

for Jim

Notice
among us how
the Thriae swarm
the reed

how
dipping low
they bind in waves
the parts
they can make music of.

How we,
raucous changelings
of the dream,
Melissae,

undo the stone
to which Her limbs
were bound

that now let fly
the bees.

THE SPIRIT MERCURY

. . . and to the barren trees
what will you say, where trust

when the last wild berry
has fallen to snow

will you say

> "he is found in the vein
> swollen with blood"

will you taste of water
that does not wet the hand?

TAKING HELEN'S BEES

It was dark in the bar. I stood next to a woman.

You know the type;
blue cloak, crescent moon hat
snake oil on wrists
red undershirt,
one of those authentic oracles
who claim to be
wilderness itself,

slightly righteous.

    "What happened to your husband?" she asked
    "He became feudal," I said. "My mind is older."

and then

    "What's that round globe on the top of your staff?"
    I asked her. "A hive," she said. "And how are the kids?"

    "Fine," I said, "I guess.
    Who are you and why the questions?"

    "I am," she said, "the Beloved of One who asks."

    "O great!" I said remembering this was California.

But she had turned silent in the way
that makes beauty serious. You know,
mysterious deep set eyes, the slow
Mediterranean turn of head . . .

". . . Look," I said, "no more questions . . ."

but she had moved closer already
and pressing me to the bar
she whispered now

"How much do you know about Troy?"

"Troy?" I gasped. "Why, only what some say.
That it was done for a song."

"Good," she said. "Here are Helen's bees."

And she was gone.

THE WINE

What lifts my hand
to warm stone
has lifted the grape
into wine.

An edition of 750 copies set in 11 point
Baskerville II at Archetype West, printed
by Thomson-Shore, Inc.,
and published by
Tooth of Time Books
634 E. Garcia
Santa Fe
New Mexico
87501

*

Grateful
acknowledgement
to the National Endowment
for the Arts
for their kind assistance

*

We encourage bookstores
to order direct from our distributors:
Bookpeople: 2929 Fifth St., Berkeley, CA 94710
Bookslinger: 213 East Fourth St., St. Paul, MN 55101
Small Press Distribution: 1814 San Pablo Ave., Berkeley, CA 94702

Julia Connor

(303) 449-0961

1634 Pine St

Boulder CO 80302